Power to the Paddle

Exercises to Improve your Canoe and Kayak Paddling

by

John Chase

To Kellie, Rachael, and Sara for making my every day brighter and putting up with my adventure antics. The best part of any trip is coming home to you. I am thankful for every day together. I love you.

Acknowledgements

I owe a big debt of gratitude to my Mom and Dad for encouraging and supporting me through the years. You opened my eyes to many cool places and helped me discover my passion for the outdoors. You started all this craziness and I thank you for doing so.

Thank you to my friends, paddling partners, personal training clients, and students I have instructed. Each of you has helped me be a better trainer and teacher and you keep me motivated to continue improving.

Thank you to my friend Brenda for taking the pictures in this book and for providing editing support.

Table of Contents

Read this first!

Disclaimer:

You must get your physician's approval before beginning this exercise program. The recommendations in this and any other document are not medical guidelines but are for educational purposes only. You must consult your physician prior to starting this or any other program or if you have any medical condition or injury that can possibly worsen with physical activity. This program is designed for healthy individuals 18 years and older only. The information in this document is meant to supplement, not replace, proper exercise training. All forms of exercise pose some inherent risks. John Chase, or anyone associated with PaddlingExercises.com or InspiredJourneyFitness.com advises readers to take full responsibility for their safety and know their limits. Before partaking in the exercises in this or any other program, be sure that your equipment is well-maintained, and do not take risks beyond your level of experience, aptitude, training and fitness. The exercises and programs in this book are not intended as a substitute for any exercise routine or treatment or regimen that may have been prescribed by your physician, physical therapist, or any other qualified professional. Do not lift heavy weights if you are alone, inexperienced, injured, or fatigued. Do not perform any exercise unless you have been shown the proper technique by a certified fitness trainer or certified strength and conditioning specialist. Always ask for instruction and assistance when lifting. Do not perform any exercise without proper instruction. Always perform a warm up prior to any exercise including but not limited to interval training. See your physician before starting any exercise or nutrition program. If you are taking any medications, you must talk to your physician before starting any exercise program, including but not limited to those in this book or at PaddlingExercises.com or InspiredJourneyFitness.com. If you experience any lightheadedness, dizziness, or shortness of breath while exercising, stop the movement and consult a physician immediately. You must have a complete physical examination if you are sedentary, if you have high cholesterol, high blood pressure, or diabetes, if you are overweight, or if you are over 30 years old. Please discuss all nutritional changes with your physician or a registered dietician. If your physician recommends that you do not use this or any other program, please follow your doctor's orders. By continuing further, you accept full responsibility for your actions.

Preface

You love to paddle. If you are like many canoeists or kayakers, you would be in a boat every day if you could. All that paddling catches up with your body though and parts you did not even know you had can start to ache. When you hurt, you tend to move less, and that means doing less of what you love...paddling. That is why I decided to write this book. I hope you enjoy it as much as I have enjoyed writing it.

My name is John Chase and I am a paddler just like you. I paddle a kayak and a canoe, but I will admit that I do favor my kayak. In addition to paddling for fun, I lead group trips and teach kayak classes. Like most paddlers, I enjoy developing my skills and introducing others to the joys of the sport. I love how paddling has offered me opportunities to connect with quiet and wild places and the chance to create memories with my family and friends to last a lifetime. I am betting that those are some of the reasons many of you paddle too.

One of my talents is teaching people to use their bodies to perform better. I am certified as a Personal Trainer through the National Academy of Sports Medicine and an ACA Certified Kayak Instructor. I have been paddling since 2002 and training clients since 2008. Throughout the past 30 years, I have had the opportunity to ride and race BMX, mountain, and road bikes throughout the US and in Europe. I have climbed through the Rocky Mountains in both summer and winter conditions, hiked through the Wasatch Range, reached the summit of Mt. Rainier, and led an expedition to climb Mexico's volcanoes. I have also participated in nearly 100 adventure races ranging from four hours to eight days in length. I have had quite a varied athletic background and I intend to pursue an adventurous lifestyle for years to come.

All these experiences have come because I have worked on gaining and maintaining my fitness levels and I have remained healthy and injury free. With this book, I will show you how to begin your own fitness program and create a stronger and more powerful paddler.

Thanks for picking up and reading this book. I hope you are able to put these tools to use and enjoy your time on the water as much as I have!

John Chase

NASM Personal Trainer

http://www.paddlingexercises.com

john@paddlingexercises.com

Why should you read this book?

Many of the paddlers I meet dream of great adventures but are often physically unprepared for the challenge. When I first began paddling I found that I wore down faster than I would have liked, despite all my other activities.

My shoulders ached. My back hurt. I was constantly shifting my legs inside the cockpit of my kayak. I was not able to get enough rotation from my body when drawing the paddle through the water. I quickly learned that although I was fit in many ways, paddling was a whole different ballgame and required that I train in different ways to meet the challenge.

The concepts and exercises in this book have helped me be a better paddler and they can make a difference for you too. These exercises will give you a foundation to stand up to the unique demands that paddling throws at you.

The pages ahead will focus on helping you:

- Sit more upright in your seat

- Reduce tension in your shoulders and low back

- Use the power of your torso to create leverage to use less energy with each stroke

- Have the endurance to handle long days in the boat

- Drive through the toughest waves or whitewater

- Protect your body against common paddling injuries

- Improve your balance and agility (so you will capsize less)

- Use force generated from your lower body to make your paddling stroke more efficient

- Carry your boat more comfortably when portaging

- While you are at it, you might even lose a few pounds. And who wouldn't mind that?

So, let's get right to it.

Types of exercise and their benefits

The first river you paddle runs through the rest of your life. It bubbles up in pools and eddies to remind you who you are. -- Lynn Noel

The three primary benefits you are looking to get from exercise are:

- **Flexibility and mobility**: Strength and endurance will not get you anywhere if you are hurt. Strong and pliable muscles moving the way the body is designed to move help keep you safe and protected from long-term damage. Repetitive stress injuries are all too common among paddlers and frequently result from relying too much on some muscles and not allowing others to share the load. If you cannot move efficiently, your body will begin to compensate. Muscles that are less suited to the task at hand will take over. When this happens, those sub-optimal muscles that are trying to accomplish that task get overloaded and begin to break down.

- **Endurance**: This is defined as the ability to perform an activity at a moderate level of exertion without exhaustion for an extended period of time. Endurance can refer to both the ability of your cardiovascular system to handle the demands placed upon it as well as the ability of your muscles to continuously perform without reaching exhaustion. For example, picture yourself having to power across a stretch of open water without stopping for an extended period of time. You are driving through some lumpy water and it is tough going, but it is not pushing you to your limit. Instead, your breathing rate increases and you are feeling the effort, but you can still hold a conversation with someone else in your boat, although the conversation is a bit choppy. That is endurance paddling. Poor endurance will leave you huffing and puffing and can possibly place you in danger.

- **Strength**: Having the physical capability to move against some type of resistance. This includes pushing, pulling, or lifting an external object or objects as well as moving your own body weight through space.

To achieve these three benefits, you will generally use a combination of flexibility and mobility movements, cardiovascular exercise, and resistance exercise. Each has their own purpose and each is important to an outdoor athlete. Many people tend to focus on only one type of exercise and exclude others. As an outdoor athlete, you need all three types to be at your peak.

Flexibility and mobility

Moving your body through a full range of motion is critical when in a canoe or kayak. Imagine if you were not able to reach forward and dip your paddle, draw the blade back to your hip, and return it with fluidity. Picture someone sitting in the bow of a canoe with their partner expecting them to be the engine that propels the boat forward. That person is unable to rotate their torso to get the blade in the water ahead of them. Without good flexibility and

dynamic range of motion, that could be you.

Flexibility is defined as the ability of the muscle to move through a full range of motion. Our bodies are meant to move through a full range of motion. Let's go through an example.

Extend your arms straight in front of you with your elbows completely straight as shown on the previous page. Your outstretched arms should be parallel to the floor with your hands in front of you. Now, bend your arms at the elbows until you have a 90 degree bend at the elbows and your hands and forearms are now perpendicular to the floor. The muscles that just made that movement happen are your biceps. You have just demonstrated a partial range of motion of the biceps.

Go ahead and repeat the same movement, but instead of stopping when your hands and forearms are perpendicular to the ground, continue to bring them backward toward your shoulders. Once you have brought your arms as far back as you can, return to that straight position with your arms and hands in front of your body with your elbows locked straight. Now you have demonstrated a full range of motion of the biceps.

Why is that important? You need to be able to move your whole body through the full range of motion to get the greatest benefit of the power of the muscle.

Dynamic range of motion is the ability of the muscles to move through a full range of motion and the nervous system's ability to effectively control the range of motion.

Just because you have the flexibility to move through that full range does not always mean you can do so properly and efficiently while protecting yourself from injury.

Cardiovascular endurance

Cardiovascular exercise, "cardio" for short, also places a load on the body, but in a different way. Many people think of cardio as the path to weight loss and see it as an endless slog on a treadmill. It is much more than that.

First off, cardiovascular exercise is intended to develop the heart, vascular system, and lungs to effectively pump blood and oxygen throughout your body.

- A rich blood and oxygen supply keeps your body functioning at peak efficiency
- Your muscles extend and contract faster and with greater force when supplied with enough oxygen
- You can move for a longer period of time before reaching exhaustion
- Better cardiovascular fitness allows you to work at a higher heart rate, producing more energy, for a longer period of time without reaching exhaustion

- You experience less fatigue when performing normal everyday life functions

- You will have a lower risk of heart disease and other complications from poor cardiovascular health

Muscular Strength

Muscular strength is developed when you place a load on the body while taking the muscles through their full range of motion. This is referred to as resistance exercise. Resistance exercise is the part that many people consider "the workout".

With resistance exercise, you are loading the muscles to create an alarm reaction, signaling a need for increased oxygen and blood supply. After repeated bouts of resistance exercise, the body adapts to handle that load by recruiting more muscle fibers. To continue to develop, once you have adapted to a stressor, you need to place a higher load on the body. This load can come in the form of more weight, lower or higher repetitions, or changing the speed at which the weight is moved. This entire process is called the Principle of Adaptation. In plain English, this means that you are shocking the body when you lift heavy stuff. The "hurt" you feel a few hours after the workout is the body telling you that you have put a load on it that it was not expecting and now your body is trying to recover so it can be strong enough to handle that load the next time.

This is a good place to note that while both resistance and cardiovascular exercise is beneficial, you can only place a certain amount of load on the body for so much time before it begins to break down. Taking calculated breaks from hard training is important and will be discussed later as we get into program design.

Developing Flexibility and Mobility

A man of wisdom delights in water. – Confucius

I talked earlier about the importance of good flexibility and mobility to a paddler.

While you may not think of these as traditional exercises, their importance cannot be overlooked. If you cannot move efficiently and control that movement effectively, you will not be at your best on the water. This section is going to take you through a series of exercises that will help improve your ability to move muscles through a full range of motion, and control that movement effectively.

Self-Myofascial Release

I would like to introduce you to one of my favorite tools to develop flexibility: the foam roller. The foam roller allows you to perform a technique known as self-myofascial release. Basically it is a self-massage. This tool works great when you have a muscle that has excess tension, sometimes referred to as a "knot". Through self-myofascial release, you are applying additional tension to a muscle that is already under tension. Ultimately, that muscle realizes that it is not going to snap and it relaxes. You can use self-myofascial release on all of the major muscle groups, but the muscle group that I will focus on first is the hamstrings.

The hamstrings are the first to go on many people. I mentioned this one earlier when talking about my own experience with my legs in my kayak.

If your hamstrings are tight, you will not be able to sit properly in your boat. Without proper hip mobility, you will not be able to develop a proper lean from the waist which means you cannot have full use of your torso as a lever to create force. Force that allows you to power your boat efficiently.

When your hamstrings have sufficient flexibility, you can sit in your boat more comfortably and you can exert better control with your feet. Moving at the hip joint, rotating the shoulders and torso, rather than rounding your back and dropping your shoulders forward is much more efficient because you are using your body as a lever.

Visit the Power to the Paddle Resources page at
http://www.paddlingexercises.com/power-to-the-paddle-
resources/ for a video to show you exactly how to use the foam
roller to loosen the hamstrings.

Mobility through the rest of the body is just as critical to being a
successful and happy paddler.

Let's look at another example.

As you are reading this, I assume you are sitting in a chair. Now,
sit on the floor with your legs straight in front of you and imagine
yourself in a kayak. Hold an imaginary paddle. Without moving
your torso, begin paddling. All you are doing here is using the
power of your arms and shoulders. Your stroke is limited by how
far you can move your arms and by the force you can generate
from your arms alone.

Now you are going to take another stroke, but this time you are
going to rotate your right shoulder forward as you bring the right
side blade toward your toes and dip it into the water. With your

blade firmly planted in the water, draw the paddle blade back by rotating your right shoulder toward the back of the boat and bring your left shoulder toward the bow, all with only a slight bend of your elbow. When the right side blade is at your hip, remove the blade from the water.

With the first stroke, you are using only your arms for power during the stroke. In the second example, you are using your arms to hold the paddle but the large muscles of the midsection, your core, are doing the work. You are using the power of your entire body and specifically, taking advantage of the leverage you can create with your body. Proper mobility along with core stability and strength made that movement happen.

Static stretching

Static stretching is the type of stretching where you stretch and hold at the point where you feel tension.

The best time to use static stretching is when you have a muscle that has excess tension. This is not unlike when you will use foam rolling to loosen a tight muscle. The old adage that you should always stretch before exercise has been shown to be less effective than historically thought. In fact, depending on the intensity of activity about to be performed, it has been determined that excessive static stretching can weaken a muscle's output. (http://www.ncbi.nlm.nih.gov/pubmed/23207883)

To perform it correctly, you will use smooth motions rather than bouncing, jerky action. Imagine pulling on the ends of a rubber band slowly so it stretches to the point where there is tension. You hold at the end of the range of motion, and then relax the band. This is how you want to perform a static stretch rather than repeatedly and rapidly yanking on the band.

If you have a specific need to relax a muscle under excessive tension or prepare muscles that have been chronically injured, here are a few sample stretches that can prove valuable.

Shoulder stretch

1. Hold your right arm straight and bring that arm across to your left side

2. Pull your right arm closer to your body by wrapping your left arm around the front of your right arm

3. Hold in this position for approximately 15-20 seconds

4. Repeat with the opposite arm

Bicep stretch

1. Hold your right arm straight out to the right side and grasp a stationary object

2. Push the right shoulder forward until you feel a slight stretch in the front of your shoulder, bicep, and chest

3. Hold in this position for approximately 15-20 seconds

4. Repeat with the opposite arm

Tricep stretch

1. Raise your right arm over your head

2. Place your right hand on your back between your shoulder blades

3. Using your left hand, lightly pull on your raised right elbow to feel a slight stretch in the triceps on your right arm

4. Hold in this position for approximately 15-20 seconds

5. Repeat with the opposite arm

Wrist extensor/flexor stretch

1. Hold your right arm in front of you with your palm facing up

2. Using your left hand, grasp the fingers of your right hand and pull back lightly until you feel a slight stretch

3. Hold in this position for approximately 15-20 seconds

4. Repeat with the opposite arm

Lat stretch

1. Reach your right arm above your head and grab a stationary object

2. Pull down lightly until you feel a slight stretch

3. Hold in this position for approximately 15-20 seconds

4. Repeat with the opposite arm

Upper back stretch

1. Extend your arms straight in front of you

2. Clasp your hands together as shown in the picture

3. Attempt to pull your hands apart from one another

4. Hold in this position for approximately 15-20 seconds

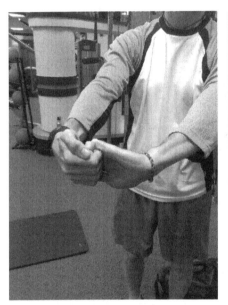 

Child's pose

1. Kneel on the floor with your hands planted on the floor in front of you

2. Sit back on your heels and stretch your arms in front of you

3. Hold in this position for approximately 15-20 seconds

Hamstring and calf stretch

1. Stand in front of a stationary object with your feet parallel to each other and separated by approximately 2 feet

2. Straighten your front leg

3. Straighten your rear leg and press your heel toward the floor

4. Lean your upper body closer to the floor until you feel a slight stretch in the hamstring of the front leg and calf of the rear leg

5. Hold in this position for approximately 15-20 seconds

6. Repeat this with the opposite leg

Quadricep stretch

1. Stand tall with a stationary object to your left side

2. Hold that object with your left hand

3. Kick your left foot behind you and grab your foot with your right hand

4. Press the left hip forward lightly until you feel a slight stretch in the left quadriceps

5. Hold in this position for approximately 15-20 seconds

6. Repeat on the opposite side

Mobility exercises

Using the foam roller and appropriate static stretching are only part of your overall flexibility and mobility program. Before going through the exercises in the other sections of this book or before putting in at your favorite paddling spot, take five minutes to warm up and get yourself ready. These dynamic mobility drills are designed to move your muscles through their full range of motion and prepare you for the activity you are about to perform. These movements may not all be needed at all times. Instead, take a few minutes to think about the activity you are about to perform and the muscles that will be used and match dynamic movements to warm up properly.

The following are several movements that I find particularly well suited to paddlers.

Head turns

1. Stand tall and turn the head
   slowly from side to side as far as
   possible without moving your
   shoulders. Perform 10
   repetitions per side

Arm circles

1. Stand tall and begin with your arms straight down by your sides

2. Rotate your arm slowly in a clockwise direction drawing a large circle. Perform 10 repetitions

3. Repeat in a counterclockwise direction. Perform 10 repetitions

High pull

1. Stand tall and begin with your arms extended in front of you

2. Forcefully pull the hands and elbows back while feeling the muscles of your upper back contract. Keep the hands and elbows at shoulder height through this exercise. Perform 10 repetitions

Traffic cop

1. Stand tall with your upper arms roughly parallel to the floor and lower arms hanging toward the floor. You should be in a classic scarecrow position

2. Rotate the shoulders to bring the hands to an upright position. Think of a robber with his hands up

3. Perform 10 rotations to the top and bottom

Thoracic spine rotation

1. Begin on the floor in a four-point position with your hands below your shoulders and knees below your hips

2. Bring one hand up and place it behind your head. (see next page)

3. Rotate that elbow and shoulder toward the ceiling without rotating your hips. Perform 10 rotations

4. Repeat on the opposite side

Bird dog

1. Begin on the floor in a four-point position with your hands below your shoulders and knees below your hips

2. Slowly extend the right arm and left leg simultaneously, attempting to bring the arm and leg parallel to the floor in a straight line with your torso. Pause at the top for 2 seconds

3. Return to the start position and repeat a total of 10 times

4. Repeat 10 times with the left arm and right leg

Fire hydrant

1. Begin on the floor in a four-point position with your hands below your shoulders and knees below your hips

2. Slowly raise the right knee directly to the side as high as possible without raising your hip or rotating your torso

3. Slowly return to the start position. Perform this movement a total of 10 times

4. Repeat with the left knee

Squat to stand

1. Squat down and grab your heels

2. Slowly stand while keeping your hands on your heels. Stand until you feel tension but do not go as far as feeling any pain!

3. Perform this movement a total of 10 times

Spiderman crawl

1. Begin standing tall

2. Lunge forward with your left leg and plant both hands on the floor to the right of your left foot

3. Release the left hand from the floor and rotate the hand toward the ceiling. Keep your eyes on your hand through the entire movement to encourage rotation of the torso

4. Pause with your hand at the top

5. Slowly lower the hand to the ground

6. Stand up on the left leg while bringing the right foot (rear foot) next to your left foot

7. Repeat the movement by lunging forward with the right foot

8. Perform this movement a total of 10 times per side

Straight arm torso rotation

1. Stand tall with your arms extended directly in front of you holding a straight object (i.e. paddle, broomstick, etc.)

2. Slowly rotate the shoulders as far as possible to your right side without turning your hips

3. Return to the start position

4. Perform this movement a total of 10 times per side

Cat and cow

1. Begin on the floor in a four-point position with your hands below your shoulders and knees below your hips

2. Slowly arch your back like an angry cat. Pause in the arched position for two seconds

3. Slowly drop your stomach to the floor to create reverse arch. Pause for two seconds in this position

4. Repeat a total of 10 times in each of the two positions

Lateral leg raises

1. Begin lying on the floor on your side. Your right elbow should be propping up your body and the elbow should be directly below the shoulder

2. Keep your legs straight. Slowly raise the top leg, driving the heel toward the ceiling. Pause at the top for 2 seconds

3. Perform this movement a total of 10 times

4. Repeat 10 times on the opposite side

Clams

1. Begin lying on the floor on your side. Your right elbow should be propping up your body and the elbow should be directly below the shoulder

2. Bend your knees creating a 90 degree angle with your feet behind you

3. Keep the feet together and slowly raise the top knee. Pause at the top for 2 seconds

4. Slowly lower the knee

5. Perform this movement 10 times

6. Repeat 10 times on the opposite side

Donkey kicks

1. Begin on the floor in a four-point position with your hands below your shoulders and knees below your hips

2. Slowly extend the right leg behind you with only a slight bend to your knee. Drive the heel toward the ceiling without allowing your back to move. Pause for 2 seconds at the top of the movement

3. Perform this movement 10 times and repeat with the left leg

Donkey whips

1. Begin on the floor in a four-point position with your hands below your shoulders and knees below your hips

2. Slowly extend the right leg behind you with only a slight bend to your knee. Drive the heel toward the ceiling without allowing your back to move. Pause for 2 seconds at the top of the movement

3. Keep your leg straight and bring your foot out to your right side while keeping

the foot off the floor.

Perform this movement

without raising the hip.

Pause at the side

4. Return the foot to the

   extended position

   behind you and then

   slowly lower back to the

   floor

5. Repeat this movement 10 times

6. Switch to the opposite side and perform 10 times

Hurdle trail leg

1. Stand tall and place your hands on a stationary object

2. Lift the right leg and drive the knee up high. This is the start position

3. Make large circles with the leg as though your feet were on the pedals of a bicycle

4. Perform 10 revolutions

5. Switch legs and perform 10 revolutions on the opposite side

Lateral leg swings

1. Stand tall and place your hands on a stationary object

2. Keep your legs straight and raise your right foot out to your right side. Keep your hips stable. Only the leg should move

3. Swing the right leg in front of your body, crossing over the left leg. Perform the exercise with no movement in the upper body and little to no rocking of the hips

4. Perform this movement 10 times

5. Repeat 10 times on the opposite side

Sagittal leg swings

1. Stand tall and place your hands on a stationary object

2. Keep your legs straight and extend your right leg behind you

3. Swing the right leg in front of your body. Perform the exercise with no movement in the upper body and little to no rocking of the hips

4. Perform this movement 10 times

5. Repeat 10 times on the opposite side

Woodpecker

1. Begin standing tall with the feet next to each other

2. Slowly extend the left leg behind you while lowering the torso. Keep a straight line from your head to your toes and work on getting your body parallel to the floor while balancing on the right leg. It is OK to perform this with the arms hanging below you or at your sides for added balance (think of airplane wings). Pause for 2 seconds in the lowered position

3. Return to a full standing position. Make sure you are standing tall at the finish with your hips forward

4. Repeat a total of 10 times

5. Switch and repeat 10 times on the opposite side

Developing Cardiovascular Endurance

Believe me, my young friend, there is nothing- absolutely nothing- half so much worth doing as simply messing about in boats. -- Kenneth Grahame from Wind in the Willows

The basis for cardio exercise is raising your heart rate to a high enough level to elicit a reaction from the body. Too low and you receive little benefit. Too high and you reach exhaustion very quickly.

Everyone has a pre-determined maximum heart rate. You cannot change your maximum heart rate, but you can change your body's ability to work closer to that maximum rate. Aside from going through a lab monitored heart rate test, which costs hundreds of dollars, there are many formulas used to estimate your max heart rate. Knowing your maximum heart rate is important because it helps you understand where you should be training to achieve the greatest benefit.

I will assume that you are an average paddler reading this with the intention of improving your cardiovascular health, and that you do not need training advice at such a scientific level that you will be prepared for the Olympics. There is some correlation between age and your max heart rate (MHR) and there are many formulas used to determine your max heart rate.

All of the formulas should be expected to have some margin of error because not everyone is built the exact same way. The following formula was developed by USA researchers, Jackson, et al (2007) and will work for our purposes:

$$MHR = 206.9 - (0.67 \text{ x age})$$

This means that a 40 year old would have a max heart rate of 180

$$180 = 206.9 - (0.67 \text{ x } 40)$$

The next step is to determine your target training heart rates that will give you the greatest cardiovascular benefit.

The chart below provides a rough estimate of the ranges determined to provide different benefits.

Age	MHR	60%	70%	80%
18	195	117	137	156
19	194	116	136	155
20	194	116	136	155
21	193	116	135	154
22	192	115	134	154
23	192	115	134	154
24	191	115	134	153
25	190	114	133	152
26	190	114	133	152
27	189	113	132	151
28	188	113	132	150
29	188	113	132	150
30	187	112	131	150
31	186	112	130	149
32	186	112	130	149
33	185	111	130	148
34	184	110	129	147
35	184	110	129	147
36	183	110	128	146
37	182	109	127	146

Age	MHR	60%	70%	80%
38	182	109	127	146
39	181	109	127	145
40	180	108	126	144
41	180	108	126	144
42	179	107	125	143
43	178	107	125	142
44	178	107	125	142
45	177	106	124	142
46	176	106	123	141
47	176	106	123	141
48	175	105	123	140
49	174	104	122	139
50	174	104	122	139
51	173	104	121	138
52	172	103	120	138
53	172	103	120	138
54	171	103	120	137
55	170	102	119	136
56	170	102	119	136
57	169	101	118	135
58	168	101	118	134
59	168	101	118	134
60	167	100	117	134

Age	MHR	60%	70%	80%
61	166	100	116	133
62	166	100	116	133
63	165	99	116	132
64	164	98	115	131
65	164	98	115	131
66	163	98	114	130
67	162	97	113	130
68	162	97	113	130
69	161	97	113	129
70	160	96	112	128
71	160	96	112	128
72	159	95	111	127
73	158	95	111	126
74	158	95	111	126
75	157	94	110	126
76	156	94	109	125
77	156	94	109	125
78	155	93	108	124
79	154	92	108	123
80	153	92	107	123
81	153	92	107	122
82	152	91	106	122
83	151	91	106	121

Age	MHR	60%	70%	80%
84	151	90	105	120
85	150	90	105	120
86	149	90	104	119
87	149	89	104	119
88	148	89	104	118
89	147	88	103	118
90	147	88	103	117

Armed with this information, you can now determine the training heart rate range that will provide the best result for your goal.

Training goal	HR %
Heart healthy	50-60%
Maximum fat metabolism	60-70%
Cardiovascular endurance	70-80%
Performance training	80-90%
Red zone	90-100%

Depending on your training plan for the day and your overall goals, you will use a combination of these ranges. As your fitness levels increase, you will have a greater capacity to reach and work within the higher ranges.

Following is a summary of the benefits you should expect to receive in each range:

- **Heart Healthy – 50-60%** – This is considered to be the best range for those just beginning their exercise program. You will begin to receive cardiovascular health benefits, start to see fat loss, lower cholesterol, and improved endurance.

- **Maximum fat metabolism – 60-70%** – This range will increase the challenge slightly and elevate your breathing rate. You will receive an added benefit with this range providing the highest percentage of calories burned coming from fat instead of stored carbohydrate. Keep in mind though that the total number of calories burned is relatively small due to the low intensity of the exercise.

- **Cardiovascular endurance – 70-80%** – Your breathing is starting to get labored and talking is becoming a bit more challenging. In this range you will develop better cardiovascular endurance so you can perform your favorite activity longer without reaching failure.

- **Performance training- 80-90%** – Breathing is very hard here and talking with someone takes quite an effort. At the top end of this range, you are completely out of breath. In this range, you are preparing your cardiovascular system to handle intense bouts of activity. Your muscles are burning from the accumulation of lactic acid. Your muscles cannot take in oxygen fast enough to clear the lactic acid and your muscles are about to shut down. You will not be able to sustain this level of intensity for long, but you will burn the most total calories and develop the ability to work closer to your maximum heart rate.

- **Red Zone – 90-100%** – You are maxing out here. You will only go into this zone if you are an elite athlete training for the highest level of athletic performance.

The preferred and most portable way to measure your heart rate and determine if you are working in the right training zones is by using a personal heart rate monitor. I use a Polar brand heart rate monitor and have used one for many years. You will find a wide range of monitors from those that only measure your heart rate to those that incorporate alarms to indicate when you are in specific zones, double as bike or running computers, and even include GPS features that can be superimposed over Google Maps to show your route.

A less portable way to monitor your heart rate is to rely on the monitors built into most home and commercial cardio training equipment. The downside here is that you are usually required to hold on to the machine, which as a trainer I do not advise. Holding on to a treadmill places you in an unnatural position and pulls your shoulders out of alignment, creating postural imbalances and leading to injury. The other downside is that it requires you to be inside. The advantage of cardio training equipment is that you can control the speed and other variables to make sure you are getting benefit from your training. It also eliminates weather related excuses that can get in the way of your training. No more "I don't want to run / ride / row / climb / whatever because it's raining outside".

An option that does not require any equipment, but is a bit more subjective, is to use Rate of Perceived Exertion to gauge your intensity and your heart rate range. Rate of Perceived Exertion (RPE) uses a scale from 1 to 20 and you estimate where you are within that range, with 1 being lying comfortably on the couch reading a book (maybe this book) and 20 being something like the feeling where you are running from an angry, hungry bear. The chart below matches RPE equivalents to the previously defined heart rate ranges

Training goal	HR %	RPE
Heart healthy	50-60%	10-11
Maximum fat metabolism	60-70%	12-13
Cardiovascular endurance	70-80%	14-16
Performance training	80-90%	16-17
Red zone	90-100%	18-20

Building a Cardiovascular Exercise Plan

Be like a duck. Calm on the surface, but always paddling

like the dickens underneath. -- Michael Caine

Many people make the mistake of jumping in to exercise at too high of an intensity for too much time.   They often start at a low intensity but quickly decide it is too easy and they drive up the length and intensity too quickly only to find injury creeping in.

Here is a sample of a 12-week cardiovascular endurance program designed for an apparently healthy person with no pre-existing conditions:

Sample 12-week cardio endurance program

Week 1

- Sunday: 20 min. @ 50-60% MHR
- Wednesday: 20 min. @ 50-60% MHR
- Friday: 20 min. @ 50-60% MHR

Week 2

- Sunday: 20 min. @ 60% MHR
- Wednesday: 20 min. @ 50-60% MHR

- Friday: 20 min. @ 60% MHR

Week 3

- Sunday: 25 min. @ 60-65% MHR
- Wednesday: 25 min. @ 60-65% MHR
- Friday: 25 min. @ 60-65% MHR

Week 4

- Sunday: 20 min. @ 60% MHR
- Wednesday: 20 min. @ 60% MHR
- Friday: 20 min. @ 60% MHR

Week 5

- Sunday: 25 min. @ 70% MHR
- Tuesday: 25 min. @ 70% MHR
- Thursday: 25 min. @ 70% MHR
- Saturday: 25 min. @ 70% MHR

Week 6

- Monday: 25 min. @ 70% MHR

- Wednesday: 25 min. @ 75% MHR

- Friday: 25 min. @ 70% MHR

Week 7

- Sunday: 30 min. @ 70% MHR

- Tuesday: 30 min. @ 70% MHR

- Thursday: 30 min. @ 70% MHR

- Saturday: 30 min. @ 70% MHR

Week 8

- Monday: 25 min. @ 65% MHR

- Wednesday: 25 min. @ 65% MHR

- Friday: 25 min. @ 65% MHR

Week 9

- Sunday: 30 min. @ 75% MHR

- Tuesday: 30 min. @ 80% MHR

- Thursday: 30 min. @ 75% MHR

- Saturday: 30 min. @ 80% MHR

Week 10

- Monday: 30 min. @ 80% MHR

- Wednesday: 30 min. @ 75% MHR

- Friday: 30 min. @ 80% MHR

Week 11

- Sunday: 35 min. @ 75% MHR

- Tuesday: 35 min. @ 80% MHR

- Thursday: 35 min. @ 75% MHR

- Saturday: 35 min. @ 80% MHR

Week 12

- Monday: 30 min. @ 70% MHR

- Wednesday: 30 min. @ 70% MHR

- Friday: 30 min. @ 70% MHR

You can make adjustments to the times in this plan depending on your existing level of endurance but keep a few things in mind:

- If developing basic endurance is your goal, increasing your heart rate above these percentages early on in your training may not be advised.

- While you may have to change the amount of time performing the exercise (duration), do not make the jumps between weeks too large. Keep the difference from week to week within the range of 5-10 minutes per session. The classic mistake people make is to feel good in the first couple of weeks when exercising for 30 minutes and immediately jump to 60 minutes. Although the cardiovascular system develops pretty quickly, the muscular system develops slower. Placing such a drastically increased load on untrained muscles significantly increases the stress and that is when injuries start to appear.

- This sample plan uses a method called "periodization". You will notice that the program increases in challenge during the first three weeks and week four brings you back down a level. It is sort of like taking three steps forward and one step backward. By giving the body that week of lighter activity, you are building in recovery time for the body to rebuild and come back stronger.

A big myth in training is that you are getting stronger WHILE you are exercising. Actually, this could not be further from the truth. You are actually getting stronger while you are recovering from exercise. That recovery time is when the body is rebuilding itself to come back stronger and handle the increase demand you are placing on it. Periodization uses rest to help you become stronger.

Developing Muscular Strength

Rivers know this: there is no hurry. We shall get there some day.-- Pooh's Little Instruction Book, inspired by A. A. Milne

Muscular strength is the ability to create force against an object or resist force placed on the body. For example, pulling a weight closer to the body or pushing a weight away from the body. This also includes training the body to resist rotation, a very important principle to the paddler. Developing muscular strength includes both core training and resistance training.

Core training

All movement begins in the core of the body. The core is most often incorrectly defined to mean the abs and when most people think of exercises for their abs, they hear "sit-ups". The core is actually the entire mid-section of the body with exception of the extremities. It includes the muscles of the chest, back, hips, glutes, hamstrings, and yes, the abs.

Core training can be broken into two separate components:

- Core stability exercises: Characterized by very little movement of the spine and core musculature during the exercise
- Core strength exercises: Includes more dynamic movement through the core through a full range of motion. These exercises tend to involve more of the body with the core providing the starting point and performing a stabilizing role through the exercise.

All beginning fitness programs for the paddler should include core stability exercises combined with appropriate resistance exercise. As the core strengthens, start to incorporate core strength exercises into the programming. Consider the core to be the foundation of your house. You do not want to build a house on top of a weak foundation. The same rule applies here. The following core exercises will help you build a strong foundation first.

Core stability exercises

Plank

1. Lie face down on the floor with your elbows under your chest and hands on the floor below your face

2. Plant your toes on the floor

3. Raise your body off the floor, creating a straight line from your head to your toes. Keep your head in line with the rest of your body. Do not drop your head toward the floor

4. Make sure your elbows are positioned directly below your shoulders

5. Hold this position for 30-60 seconds

Bridge T-falloff

1. Begin seated on a stability ball

2. Walk your feet forward and bridge your body to the bridge position with, a 90 degree bend at the knees, and your head and shoulders supported by the ball

3. Stretch your arms out to the sides

4. Keeping your hips level, slowly roll the ball side to side as far as you can without falling off the ball

5. Roll to each side 8-10 times

Side plank

1. Lie on your side with your elbow directly below your shoulder and your feet stacked on top of one another

2. Raise your hip off the floor to create a straight line from your head to your feet

3. Hold this position for 30-60 seconds

4. Repeat on the opposite side

Ball rollout

1. Kneel on the floor in front of a stability ball with your hands placed on the side of the ball

2. Roll the ball forward by pivoting on your knees and without bending at the hips. Your hips, shoulders, and hands should move simultaneously. Do not allow your lower back to collapse. Roll only as far as the low back will allow

3. Pause for a few seconds and roll back to the start position

Anti-rotation press

1. Wrap a resistance band around a stationary object
2. Face sideways to the direction of pull on the band
3. Step away from the stationary object to create tension on the resistance band
4. Hold the handles of the band close to your chest

5. Push your hands away from your body to change the direction of pull.
6. Switch sides and repeat

Stir the pot

1. Place yourself in the plank position with your elbows on a stability ball

2. Slowly make small circles with your elbows, rolling the ball slightly under you

3. Hold this position for approximately 30-60 seconds

Rowing crunch

1. Lie face up on the floor with your fingers tucked under your behind

2. Press your low back hard toward the floor. Make sure your low back does not arch excessively at any time during the exercise

3. Raise your feet a few inches off the floor while keeping your legs straight

4. Slowly draw your knees toward your chest

5. Slowly return to the start position

Reverse crunch

1. Lie face up on the floor with your fingers tucked under your behind

2. Press your low back hard toward the floor. Make sure your low back does not arch excessively at any time during the exercise

3. Raise your feet a few inches off the floor while keeping your legs straight

4. Slowly raise your feet straight up above you while keeping your legs straight

5. Slowly lower your legs toward the floor without bending your legs. Do not let your feet touch the floor and make sure your back does not arch excessively at any time during the exercise

Core strength exercises

Stability ball pike

1. Begin with your hands on the floor and your feet on a stability ball. Maintain a neutral position with your back, keeping your entire body in a straight line

2. Slowly drive your hips toward the ceiling while keeping your arms and legs straight and feet balancing on the ball

3. Return to the start position

Cable side bend

1. Wrap a resistance band around a stationary object
2. Face sideways to the direction of pull on the resistance band
3. Step far enough away from the stationary object to create moderate tension on the resistance band
4. Hold the handles of the resistance bands above your head with straight arms. This is the start position

5. Slowly bend toward the stationary object to reduce the

    tension

6. Return to the start position

Reverse hyperextension

1. Lie on a bench with your hips and legs off the bench and knees below and toward the floor as shown. This is the start position

2. Slowly extend your legs behind you to create a straight line from your toes to your head

3. Slowly return to the start position

Stability ball pass

1. Lie face up on the floor with your arms stretched out on the floor over your head (see next page)

2. Press your low back hard toward the floor. Make sure your low back does not arch excessively at any time during the exercise

3. Squeeze a stability ball between your feet. This is the start position

4. Keep your legs and arms straight. Slowly raise the stability ball in the air while raising your hands toward the rising ball

5. As your hands meet the ball, grab the ball and slowly lower it toward the floor over your head

6. Stop just short of your feet and the ball touching the floor

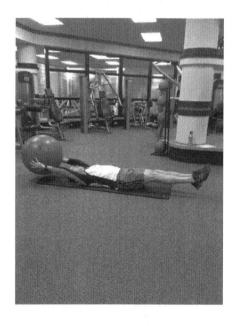

Resistance training

There are hundreds of variables to consider with weight training. Just a few examples include:

- Machine based

- Dumbbells

- Barbells

- Kettlebells

- Bodyweight

- Suspension training

- Medicine balls

- Stability balls

- Balance training

- Full-body exercise

- Upper body / lower body splits

The list goes on. All of these, and more, can be great additions to a training program. Depending on your level of comfort and conditioning, you will find that you use different tools to get the job done.

Using a variety of equipment will allow you to gain greater benefit from your program while decreasing boredom. Equipment does not have to be large and expensive to be effective. Personally, I am a big fan of portable equipment that I can take almost anywhere, including simple pieces like resistance bands and medicine balls to more effective tools like the TRX suspension trainer (learn more about the TRX Suspension Trainer at http://trx.inspiredjourneyfitness.com).

For the sake of simplicity, and assuming that you are just starting an exercise program, I will review a sequence of exercises that cover all of the basic human movements using only a set of resistance bands.

Resistance exercises

Resistance Band Chest Press

1. Loop your resistance bands around a stationary object

2. Facing away from the anchor point, hold the handles close to your armpits with your elbows behind you

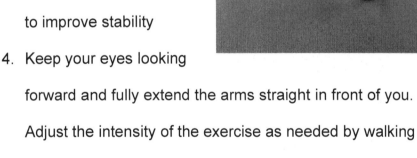

3. Stand tall with one foot slightly behind the other to improve stability

4. Keep your eyes looking forward and fully extend the arms straight in front of you. Adjust the intensity of the exercise as needed by walking farther away from or back toward the anchor point

5. Slowly return your hands to the start position with your hands near your armpits

Resistance Band Row

1. Loop your resistance bands around a stationary object

2. Facing toward the anchor point, grasp the handles and extend your hands directly in front of you

3. Stand tall with both feet next to each other and placed approximately shoulder width apart

4. Looking forward, draw your hands to your armpits with your elbows behind you. Do not allow your elbows to flare out to your sides during the movement. Adjust the intensity of the exercise as appropriate by walking farther away from or back toward the anchor point

5. Slowly return your hands to the start position with your hands extended in front of you

Resistance Band Core Rotation

1. Loop your resistance bands around a stationary object

2. Facing toward the anchor point, grasp the handles and extend your hands directly in front of you. Adjust the intensity of the exercise as appropriate by walking farther away from or back toward the anchor point

3. Your left foot should be pointing toward the anchor point. Your right foot should be behind the left slightly wider than shoulder width. The right foot should be perpendicular to the anchor point with the toes facing out

4. Keeping your arms straight, slowly rotate your hips and shoulders until you are facing away from the anchor point. While rotating, pivot on the toes of the foot that is facing

the anchor point. The motion of that foot should feel similar to the movement as if you were squishing a bug into the floor

5. Slowly return to the start position. Do not allow the resistance of the band to snap you back to the start position. You must always remain in control

6. Switch and repeat on the other side

Resistance Band Squat

1. Step on the middle of the tubing with your feet approximately shoulder width apart

2. Grasp the handles and stand tall with your hands near your shoulders. Adjust the intensity of the exercise as appropriate by spreading the feet farther away from each other or closer to each other

3. Keep your feet planted on the floor and squat down by pushing your butt backward as though you are going to sit in a chair

behind you. Do not allow the knees to drive forward and move farther forward than your toes. Initiate the movement with the knees and hips. Do not simply lower the shoulders without bending the knees. If this movement is too challenging with the band, omit the band and perform a squat using only your body weight

4. Return to the tall standing position with your hips fully forward

Resistance Band Overhead Press

1. Step on the middle of the tubing with your feet shoulder width apart.

2. Grasp the handles and stand tall with your hands near your shoulders. Adjust the intensity of the exercise by spreading the feet farther away from or closer to each other.

3. Slowly extend your arms, raising your hands directly above your shoulders

4. Slowly return to the start position with your hands near your shoulders

Resistance Band Internal Rotation

1. Loop your resistance bands around a stationary object

2. Use a light resistance band or maintain a relatively close distance to the anchor point. Adjust the intensity of the exercise as appropriate by walking farther away from or back toward the anchor point

3. Face to the right side of the anchor point and grasp both handles in the left hand

4. With your left hand pointing directly to the anchor point, keep your left elbow pinned to your side, but not digging in to your side and maintain a 90 degree bend at the elbow. You are now in the start position as shown in the first photo above

5. Keeping your left elbow at your side, slowly rotate your left hand across to the right side of your body

6. Slowly return to the start position

7. Perform this movement for the prescribed number of repetitions

8. Switch sides and repeat on the opposite side

Resistance Band External Rotation

1. Loop your resistance bands around a stationary object (see next page)

2. Use a light resistance band or maintain a relatively close distance to the anchor point. Adjust the intensity of the exercise as appropriate by walking farther away from or back toward the anchor point

3. Face to the right side of the anchor point and grasp both handles in the right hand

4. Your right hand should be across your body as shown in the first picture below. Keep your right elbow pinned to your side, but not digging in to your side and maintain a 90 degree bend at the elbow. You are now in the start position as shown in the first picture on the next page

5. Keeping your right elbow at your side, slowly rotate your right hand across to the out and away from the right side of your body

6. Slowly return to the start position

7. Perform this movement for the prescribed number of repetitions

8. Switch sides and repeat on the opposite side

Resistance Band Reverse Y-fly

1. Loop your resistance bands around a stationary object

2. Facing toward the anchor point, grasp the handles and extend your hands directly in front of you

3. Maintain straight arms with little to no bend at the elbows. Adjust the intensity of the exercise as appropriate by walking farther away from or back toward the anchor point

4. Slowly raise the arms to a "Y" position, ending with your hands out to your sides

5. Slowly return to the start position

Resistance Band Reverse T-fly

1. Loop your resistance bands around a stationary object

2. Facing toward the anchor point, grasp the handles and extend your hands directly in front of you. Adjust the intensity of the exercise as appropriate by walking farther away from or back toward the anchor point

3. Maintain straight arms with little to no bend at the elbows

4. Slowly spread the arms to a "T" position, ending with your hands out to your sides

5. Slowly return to the start position

Resistance Band Forward T-fly

1. Loop your resistance bands around a stationary object

2. Facing away from the anchor point, grasp the handles and extend your hands directly in front of you. Adjust the intensity of the exercise as appropriate by walking farther away from or back toward the anchor point

3. Maintain straight arms with little to no bend at the elbows

4. Slowly bring the arms to the sides ending in a "T" position with your hands out to your sides (see next page)

5. Slowly return to the start

   position

Resistance Band Lying Pulldown

1. Loop your resistance bands around a stationary object

2. Lie flat on the floor, face up with your head toward the anchor point and your arms extended above your head closer to the anchor point.

Adjust the intensity of the exercise as appropriate by sliding farther away from or back toward the anchor point

3. Keeping your hands and elbows on the floor, slowly pull the handles until you have a 90 degree bend at the elbows and your hands are approximately at ear level (see next page)

4. Slowly return to the start

   position

Resistance Band Seated Pulldown

1. Loop your resistance bands around a stationary object with the anchor point above your head

2. Sit on the floor with your legs in front of you and your arms extended above your head closer to the anchor point

3. Slowly pull the handles toward the floor until you have a 90 degree bend at the elbows and your hands are approximately at ear level

4. Slowly return to the start position

Building a strength training program

The rivers flow not past, but through us, thrilling,

tingling, vibrating every fiber and cell of the substance of

our bodies, making them glide and sing.- John Muir

Your resistance exercise plan, like your cardiovascular plan reviewed earlier, should be designed in a progressive fashion. We will use the periodization concept again to build progressively over the first three weeks and take a step backward on the fourth week to allow recovery.

There are many different ways to build resistance programs, as many methods as there are goals. Although many think of paddling as an upper body activity, it is truly a full body activity. Your arms hold the paddle. Your torso rotates to draw the blade through the water. Your lower body braces you in the boat. Your entire body works together as a machine to carry gear to and from the put-in and portage your boat.

To meet the unique full body demands placed on a paddler, we are going to build a program that incorporates all of the basic human movements:

- Push – pushing something away from the body (forward or overhead)

- Pull – pulling something toward the body (from front, from the floor, or from above)

- Bend – side to side or forward and back

- Rotate – turning the body on its axis

- Squat or lunge

Since paddling is a very shoulder intensive activity, I would also recommend that every paddler include basic shoulder rotation and strengthening exercises in their resistance programming.

When developing your personal program, think about each of these motions. Select an exercise from those shown in this book to match that motion and you have yourself a program.

Using this concept, here is a sample selection of exercises:

Movement	Sample Exercise
Push (forward)	Chest press
Push (overhead)	Shoulder press
Pull (from front)	Row
Pull (from floor)	Upright row
Pull (from above)	Seated pulldown
Bend	Side bends
Rotate	Core rotation
Squat or lunge	Squat

As noted above, add a shoulder internal and external rotation exercise as shown in the Resistance Exercise section.

Sets and reps

Figuring out what to do with those exercises comes next. The terminology used to describe the number of times you perform an exercise is sets and reps.

- A *rep*, or repetition, is the number of times an exercise is performed.

- A *set* is a collection of repetitions. For example, one set might contain 12 repetitions. During an exercise session, you might perform several sets of the same exercise.

Goal	Endurance	Strength
Sets	2-3	3-6
Reps	12-15	8-12
Weight	Lower	Higher

The number of sets performed, the number of repetitions in each set, and the amount of weight used for each repetition will change depending on your goals and where you are in your training plan. When you are beginning your exercise program, you need to develop basic muscular endurance. In this phase, you will use fewer sets and a higher number of repetitions. The intent here is to condition the muscle to perform the movement correctly without overemphasizing the amount of weight being used. Using a heavy weight in this phase will tend to compromise your ability to perform the exercise correctly, potentially exposing you to injury.

Using the above sample exercise selections for someone starting in the endurance phase would look like this:

Movement	Sample Exercise	Sets	Reps
Push (forward)	Chest press	2	15
Push (overhead)	Shoulder press	2	15
Pull (from front)	Row	2	15
Pull (from floor)	Upright row	2	15
Pull (from above)	Seated pulldown	2	15
Bend	Side bends	2	15
Rotate	Core rotation	2	15
Squat or lunge	Squat	2	15

After progressing through the endurance phase, you will move to a strength development phase where you will increase the number of sets and reduce the number of reps, while simultaneously increasing the weight.

Set and rep selection for someone in the endurance phase might look like this:

Movement	Sample Exercise	Sets	Reps
Push (forward)	Chest press	3-6	8-12
Push (overhead)	Shoulder press	3-6	8-12
Pull (from front)	Row	3-6	8-12
Pull (from floor)	Upright row	3-6	8-12
Pull (from above)	Seated pulldown	3-6	8-12
Bend	Side bends	3-6	8-12
Rotate	Core rotation	3-6	8-12
Squat or lunge	Squat	3-6	8-12

Conclusion

Now that you are armed with the information you need to develop your exercise plan to be a better paddler, the next step is yours to take. A few final words of wisdom:

- Consistency is key. Once you have developed your plan, you have to work the plan. The goal of both cardiovascular and strength training is to force your body to adapt to the load you place upon it. Cardio training or resistance training one time a week will not force your body to adapt. Aim for three to four days of cardio work and one to two days of strength work.
- It is OK to perform your strength work and cardio work on the same day. However, I recommend that you perform your strength work first and the cardio work last. You want your body to be at its strongest when performing resistance training.

- Always warm up prior to your main exercise session. The mobility drills in this book provide a perfect warm up to prepare the body for the main exercise session about to follow. The mobility exercises are also great options for your recovery weeks.

- You need to have a solid nutrition plan in place to gain benefit from your cardio and resistance training. That means eating well and eating enough to support your goals. This book is not intended to be a nutrition reference and I recommend that you research and obtain quality nutrition advice. Quality advice means no fad diets. Learn to eat like you are going to eat for the rest of your life.

- Focus on you rather than your gear. Paddlers are gearheads. We spend a lot of time playing with equipment. We find a new paddle with a lighter swing weight that we believe will give us that little bit of an advantage. We lust over the latest boat constructed from lightweight high-tech materials. We often forget that paying attention to our own strength to weight ratio will pay even greater dividends on the water and in daily life.

Being the best paddler you can be takes time and effort. Every moment spent developing yourself translates to a more enjoyable time on the water. The exercises and programs that I have outlined in this book have made a difference for me and many other paddlers just like you. Put these tools into action and you will have a better experience while still having the energy to swap stories at the after-paddle campfire.

Now, it's time to get to work!

You must live in the present, launch yourself on every wave, find your element in each moment. – Henry David Thoreau

See you on the water!

Appendix

Throughout this book I have referenced several charts. You can find these charts along with links to videos and other resources to help you use this book to its fullest at
http://www.paddlingexercises.com/power-to-the-paddle-resources/

Index

Also available from John Chase

Your Fitness Journey DVD gives you over 80 videos showing exercises of varying levels of difficulty in several different categories.

Unlike most fitness DVDs that give you one or two pre-determined workout programs to follow which quickly become boring and routine, you will have the opportunity to mix and match exercises and create hundreds of fun and interesting combinations. In addition, almost all of the exercises can be performed with a minimal amount of portable equipment that you probably already own!

Visit http://www.paddlingexercises.com/your-fitness-journey-dvd/ to learn more and purchase Your Fitness Journey today!

Made in the USA
Middletown, DE
11 December 2016